THE
DUFFER'S
GUIDE TO
RUGBY

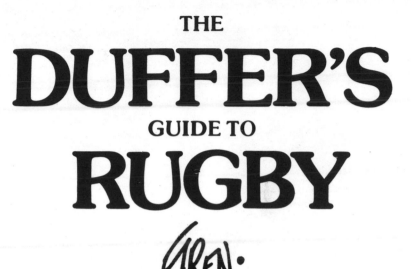

Introduction by Max Boyce

**COLUMBUS BOOKS
LONDON**

Other books in the Duffer's series:

The Official Duffer's Rules of Golf (John Noble)
The Official Duffer's Rules of Tennis (Bob Adams)
The Duffer's Guide to Golf: A Second Slice (Gren)

Forthcoming titles:

The Duffer's Guide to Cricket (Gren)

First published in Great Britain in 1984 by
Columbus Books
Devonshire House, 29 Elmfield Road, Bromley, Kent BR1 1LT

Printed and bound by
Clark Constable
Hopetoun Street, Edinburgh EH7 4NF

ISBN 0 86287 172 7

Ever since that wonderful day in 1823 at Rugby School when young William Webb-Ellis 'who, with a fine disregard for the rules of football, as played in his time, took the ball in his arms and ran with it, thus originating the distinctive feature of the Rugby game', people have been watching the game and wondering why he bothered.

With this in mind, we offer the *Duffer's Guide to Rugby* in an effort to help you view the game with greater appreciation or even inspire you to start playing it.

CONTENTS

6

Introduction

In the last few seasons Welsh Rugby has had something of a trying period following the heady days of the 'seventies when half the national side were household names and such was the interest that when a preacher asked in the Tabernacle Chapel in a West Wales village 'What would you do if Christ came back tomorrow?' a child up the back was heard to remark, 'Move Barry John into the centre!'

However, what followed was inevitable, for the wheel had turned full circle. They were worrying days and after the home defeat by Scotland a great darkness fell over the land and we all wondered what was to follow – boils or locusts? . . .

In those troubled days there still remained GREN, who more than any other I know cheered and sustained us through that difficult period. What Vera Lynn did for the forces in World War II with her songs, Gren did for Welsh rugby followers with his pencil ... a sharp, knowing, inventive pencil that has enriched the world of rugby football.

The Duffer's Guide to Rugby will, I know, appeal to the rugby fraternity all over the world, for there are duffers everywhere when and wherever the game of rugby football is played, with some twenty-three duffers in Wales spread evenly amongst the 29,000 secondary school caps!

May the ball bounce kindly for them!

7

Playing Types

Rugby players can be divided into three basic types, and are easily identified as they are seen sprinting, hiding or thumping away their Saturday afternoons.

Type 1: The decent chap

A real pain in the neck — always turns up on the right day at the right time in peak condition, even understands the set move calls and expects others around him to do so as well. He's sickeningly sporting: claps opposition tries even when his side is losing. Beware of him — he drinks orange juice and plays squash.

Type 2: The club psychopath

A decent enough chap, good to his kids and tourists and all that sort of thing, and he looks forward to his Saturday afternoons more than most.

Not for him the heady glory of the blond-maned outside half or winger idolized for his all-too-obvious efforts. The psychopath's skills often go unsung by the fans as he spends his afternoons on the ref's blind side, busily butting, groining, punching, elbowing, biting or raking.

Type 3: The I-happened-to-be-around-and-they-were-one-short type

Usually found idling away the afternoon on the wing or as far away from the action as possible. He vaguely wonders what's going on, moving only if the play comes his way, interrupting him while he was admiring the view of the village church.

He can easily be identified: he's the chap who, on accidental receipt of the ball, throws it thirty feet vertically into the air and runs off screaming.

Playing Positions —
or where to stand on the field, depending on your shape

Your playing position in rugby depends on physical proportions and personality.

For instance, a six-foot-eight introvert may be all right in the second row, but at scrum half he'd be lost.

In the same way, it's not possible to play in the front row if nature has given you anything approaching a neck.

1. The full back, No. 15

A much-sought-after position beloved by the broad-shouldered, death-or-glory-type players who enjoy getting involved in the game only when they feel like it — for instance, bursting into the line to warm themselves up after long, cold periods of inactivity. These periods of inactivity are thought by the full back to be tactical positioning in cover, while his forwards say it's keeping out of trouble.

The full back must also develop a skill which renders him obstructed by his own team, preventing him fielding a high ball after shouting a very brave, theatrical 'my ball!'.

13

2. The wings, Nos. 11 and 14

To be happy as a winger, you must have three basic qualities:
(1) speed
(2) indifference to inactivity
(3) enjoyment of chatting up girls (touch-line talent, as it's known in the trade).
Many wingers referring to their 'best games' are talking about the number of dates they have arranged, not tries scored. Recently a club record was shattered by a particularly good-looking winger who arranged five separate dates before half time and met and got engaged to someone else during the second half.

3. The centres, Nos. 12 and 13

The most shapeless of all rugby positions. Centres who are stockily built think they are crash-ball specialists while leaner-built centres are invariably outside halves who can't get in at that position and are happy to play centre until the outside half is stretchered-off, which the centre is working on by giving him a series of hospital passes.

4. The outside half, No. 10 (five eight)

Ideally, the outside half should be broad-shouldered, slim-waisted and of golden mane. If he can also play a bit, it's an advantage.

There are two kinds of outside half:
(1) the kicking type ('he kicks too much – he never gets his line going')
(2) the running/passing type ('hasn't he ever heard of tactical kicking?')

To establish yourself at outside half, you should ideally be an intelligent, athletic student of the game who's related to the chairman of the Selection Committee.

5. The scrum half, No. 9 (half back)

To be a scrum half one has to be shortish, have a very low centre of gravity and the ability to talk non-stop throughout the game, even when knocked unconscious.

The scrum half never has a bad game. If he has a stinker, it's not his fault: the forwards gave him rubbish ball and no protection.

If, however, he has a good game, it's 'Who couldn't play a blinder behind a pack like that?'

17

6. The props, Nos. 1 and 3

Props are the hairy ones you see getting up last from a collapsed scrum yet first into the club bar.

They happily grunt away the afternoon in the darkness of the scrummage, hoping to provide ball for the backs, all of whom they consider to be fairies anyway.

7. The hooker, No. 2

The beauty of being a hooker is that you always get a game because very few people want to play there.

Most clubs are bulging at the seams with outside halves and flankers, but hookers – they're lucky if they've got more than one.

Hookers are born and not made, with no neck, bandy legs and long arms.

8. Second row, Nos. 4 and 5 (lock forward)

Locks are the big, gangling, angelic-looking chaps who are there to get the retaliation going. Not for them the sly kidney punch so beloved of flankers. Locks take pride in a well-delivered blow during an early line-out, hidden from the referee's eyes only by the other lock who has to be an experienced referee-unsighter.

9. Flankers, Nos. 6 and 7 (breakaways)

Flankers are the flash ones, running about tackling everyone and generally behaving in a most unfriendly way, often deported New Zealanders.

They tend to bleed a lot and often get knocked out, emerging from the trainer's treatment swathed in bandages, dramatically determined to resist all attempts to make them leave the field.

21

10. The number eight, No. 8 (lock)

The number eight is the tallish chap who leans on the end of the scrummage and prevents the ball coming out quickly. He's usually a frustrated scrum-half, always trying to pick up a well-heeled ball and trying to dive over from five yards out — usually failing.

Rugby Club People

No matter how, on the field of play, teams may differ, the people behind the scenes are always the same, their community status may vary depending on locality, but all over the world they are the same basic types.

Any serious student of the game joining a club for the first time must learn to identify these types and act accordingly (i.e. ignore them).

1. The club chairman

Easily recognized, he's the one in the club blazer, tie and sweater, warmly welcoming any visiting committee man to the club. He's always at least four hospitality drinks ahead of anyone, and hasn't seen a game in focus since accepting the chairmanship. His rugby career was probably cut short by an over-zealous All-Black lock forward.
Nice enough chap if only he'd stop making speeches.

2. The trainer

Trainers are usually de-frocked vets who have been refused entry into the St John Ambulance and have joined the rugby club to satisfy their medical aspirations.

Many are the promising players whose careers he's halted by mis-diagnosing indigestion when it was caved-in ribs.

One case is recorded of a trainer treating a player for having had his teeth kicked in before realizing he was wearing a gumshield.

3. The committee man

He's the one with pockets bulging with raffle tickets, AGM minutes and photocopies of the latest committee notices.
Spends every night of the week working on behalf of the club – in fact, he'll do almost anything to keep away from his wife.

26

4. The coach

Funny people – seem to understand tactics and rules. They spend hours teaching set moves, then take the credit when points are scored without using them. Coaches are usually ex-internationals or vindictive traffic wardens.

27

5. The moaning fan

Hates the committee, hates the team, hates the beer, hates all New Zealanders. Thinks the club steward is on the fiddle (he probably is).
Hasn't missed a home game since 1946 and has asked for his ashes to be scattered on the club end tryline.

Referees

Each referee is biased, one-eyed, intimidated, bought, a homer or just plain stupid, according to the hundreds of fair-minded, noble, decisive, quick-witted, rule-appreciating referees on the touchline.

Referees come in four basic types...

1. The let-the-game-flow-at-all-costs type

This referee will let anything go to ensure the game swings from end to end. He does this for several reasons:

(1) he believes rugby should be a swift-moving handling exhibition;

(2) he thinks it will entertain the fans;

(3) he wants to show off how fit he is by keeping up with the players.

2. The got-a-new-whistle-for-Christmas type

Blows up at every possible opportunity, even half way through half-time (to make sure the whistle hasn't seized up).

He blows to indicate infringements, offences, to call trainers on, to send trainers off and to admonish slow-operating scoreboard attendants.

One thing in favour of this kind of ref: he's never far from the centre of play – he never lets it get more than ten yards from his last blow-up position.

31

3. The ex-military type

Tries to run the game by sheer dominance of personality – will shout at everyone, wag his finger, attempt to intimidate even the front rows. He gives the impression of being in complete control. This type of referee has only one failing – he hardly ever knows the laws.

4. The over-intelligent type

This is the most irritating type of referee. The game grinds to a halt while he discusses the implications of the laws with a transgressor and the ensuing debate becomes involved around interpretations.

He's also the only one on the field to have understood the latest amendment to some long-lost law, and will not be hurried into sending off trainers who spend ten minutes on the field tending a malingering flanker.

33

Referees' Signals Explained

To enable players and onlookers to understand why the referee is ruining what could be a wonderful, flowing game of rugby, the powers-that-be have established a series of signals for the ref to make his decisions for continually blowing-up obvious to all.

1. I'm totally confused, but something illegal must have happened.

2. Do that to my son again and I'll send you off.

3. My Auntie is in the stand.

35

4. I saw
the offence
but he's too big
for me
to send off.

5. I am the local
hokey-cokey
champion.

6. Don't
expect me to run:
my guide dog
bit me
yesterday.

7. I have just
penalized
their psychopath.

8. This is
my first game.
I want to be
sick.

9. I want
to go
to the
loo.

37

10. See me all right at half-time or I'll penalize you every ten minutes!

11. My shorts have been ripped off.

12. What the hell – it's my last game, anyway.

Tactics: Calling the Moves

The game's organizing bodies are always motivating coaches to think tactics. It is well-known that coaches are nutty enough without eager-beaver do-gooders encouraging them in their search for excellence. To this end, coaches expect their players to understand blackboard tactics, pre-conceived moves that are called usually by the most intelligent player, who is probably the outside half.

The keen student of the game, however, can read the moves just by looking at the outside half. From any line-out or set scrum there are four basic moves. They are as follows...

(1) If I Get It, I Will Kick It

(2) If I Get It, I Will Drop It

(3) If I Get It, I Will Feign Injury

**(4) If I Get It,
I Will Never Speak To You Again**

Correct Dress For Match Day

To be properly turned-out on match day is all-important in rugby; no matter if you are a player, touch judge, humble fan or even a referee, there are certain uniformities which must be adhered to...

1. The player

(1) Shirt: ideally, should match those worn by some of your side.

(2) Boots: should be large enough to hold travelling expenses.

(3) Hamstring: useful to blame when your speed starts to go.

(4) Stiff arm: for stiff-arming.

(5) Loose bootlace: always good for a minute's rest while you do it up.

(6) Permit: useful to carry with you at all times to check who you're playing for this week.

(7) Half-time pocket: handy for ciggies, lighter, poison-pen letters to ref, etc.

(8) Knee bandage: gives you the impression of being tough and experienced.

(9) Gumshield: for shielding gums after all your teeth have been knocked out.

2. The referee

(1) The shirt: ideally, this should differ in colour to that of the teams' – unless you don't care who knows you're a homer.

(2) The watch: should be liniment-proof.

(3) Another watch: in case the first watch gets stolen by shifty, bald flanker in untidy maul.

(4) The wallet: containing name and address of your next-of-kin, blood group, etc.

(5) The pen: for writing down statements which may later be used in GBH court case.

(6) The shorts: must have pockets which conceal map of fast escape route.

(7) The badge: anything impressive will do.

(8) The book of useful phrases: e.g. the Welsh for 'Oi, you! You shifty little four-eyed pillock!'

(9) The boots: always wear boots; wellies look silly.

3. The touch judge

(1) Track suit: must be faded, dirty and too small (as for ex-player of long experience).

(2) Club's name: so that there's no doubt as to which way you're biased.

(3) Beer gut: indicates to opposition that you're on the committee.

(4) Traditional gesture: opposition behind you are always one-eyed.

(5) Flag: wave it occasionally and point towards your team.

(6) Personal hi-fi and earphones: helps to pass the time.

(7) Big boots: to slow you down (touch judges overtaking wingers looks bad).

(8) Shorts: worn over track-suit bottoms if you're a Home Counties trendy touch judge.

(9) Perfect eye: to judge exactly ten yards more on your ball and ten yards less on theirs.

4. The fan

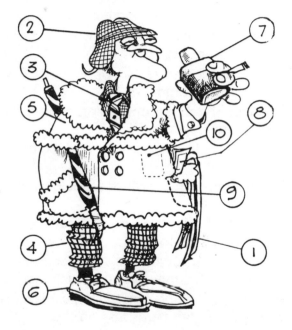

(1) Scarf: in some up-market college colours. Should always hang casually from pocket.

(2) Hat: the odder the better. Real fans never go bare-headed.

(3) Club tie: if they won't sell you a club tie, wear a white polo-neck sweater.

(4) Trousers: must be baggy, preferably cor-duroy or check.

(5) Coat: if your duffle coat has expired at last, wear anything untidy. Don't wear a British Warm unless you have committee aspirations.

(6) Wellies or Polyveldts: no self-respecting fan would wear Gucchi.

(7) Hip flask: looks impressive, and others won't know if it contains Sanatogen.

(8) Programme: pretend to check the visiting team while secretly you see who's in yours.

Types of Pass

In this section we have not covered the more ordinary type of pass, such as throwing the ball vertically into the air while screaming and running away from that hairy tackler who seems to want the ball much more than you.

1. To the left

Ideally, if using this pass, the player who you would like to receive the ball should be standing on your left.

50

2. To the right

As for passing to the left, except it would be nice for the recipient to be on your right.

51

3. The 'varsity pass

The poseur's pass: flash, textbook stuff, usually executed when your side is at least twenty points ahead with a minute to play, no physical opposition and the passer is trying to impress a bird on the touchline.

4. The reverse pass

Useful during moments of sheer terror (e.g. when confronted by your girlfriend's husband coming aggressively round the blind side) to change the direction of attack.

5. The French pass

Typical Froggie clever-dick stuff, which always seems to work for them. If you try it, they'll intercept and score. A cross between basketball and volleyball, it should never be used unless you're indispensable or related to the club chairman.

6. The spin pass

This pass is beloved of scrum halves because they are convinced that the spinning ball travels accurately and much further. You can always tell when this pass has been used: the ball can be seen spinning off the outside half's chest, his legs, his forehead...

7. The dive pass

Mainly used by flash scrum halves when being watched by country or county selectors. It should be used in dry conditions only: nothing is more guaranteed to ruin your chances with the touchline talent than the sight of your delicate, artistic dive ending up as an undignified bellyflop in a muddy pool.

8. The dropped pass

The most common of all passes: needs no great talent in execution. Many wings with no one to beat and the line gaping at their mercy employ this pass just to excite the supporters.

57

9. The flip pass

Used by chicken centres who have no desire to be holding the ball when the opposition nasty is so near. If, resulting from your flip pass, a try is scored, you will be hailed as having 'great vision', 'tactical awareness', etc.

10. The hospital pass

This pass is thrown so that it can be caught just as the opposition stiff-arming, knee-high, kidney-punching specialist is about to leap upon the recipient.

The pass should be given in selected cases only: for instance, to your wife's boyfriend or to the guy who stole your bird on the last Easter tour. You will also be the toast of the club bar if you give one to your coach when he's playing in a club veterans' friendly.

Types of Kick

Although rugby is supposed to be a handling game, kicking plays a very important part in developing attacks, clearing defence, scoring points and injuring the psychopath.

Kicking is, of course, a very basic, natural movement: the ball should be struck with the foot – ideally, the one you're not standing on.

If you can kick equally well with either foot, you shouldn't be reading this book anyway.

1. The punt

This is the frenzied kick so beloved of front-row men when, to their amazement, they receive the ball in open play. Mental panic ensues and the big, quick boot (i.e. the punt) is employed; usually, almost anywhere that the ball decides to go will do.

61

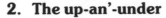

2. The up-an'-under

This is something like the punt but the ball should be kicked higher, thus giving you and your sadistic little friends time to run forward and trample all over the poor innocent who has been foolish enough to try to catch the ball. Up-and-unders are good fun: use them as often as possible.

3. The touch-finding screw kick

This kick is supposed to send the ball long and parallel to the touchline when, at the end of its travels, it gently drifts into touch.

Never attempt this kick. You'll probably boot it straight into the stand two yards away. In the highly unlikely event of the kick going where you want it to, everyone will think it's a fluke anyway.

63

4. The grubber

A low, trajectory kick designed to make the ball roll tantalizingly along the touchline before eluding a defender's grasp to bobble into touch. Well, that's all very well in theory, but what usually happens is that the grubber is mis-kicked straight into the opposition full back's hands, whereupon he runs through your side to score the winning try.

5. The chip

A beautiful, short, delicate kick in which the ball is accurately placed for you or one of your little friends to run on to.

This kick is a delight to see if executed by a player of class, when, with only the advancing full back to beat, the ball is chipped over his head and, as he is being passed, the full back's ribs are playfully smashed into our hero's fist.

6. The drop

Usually executed by the golden-maned outside half type, who considers he's the only one who can do it. The ball is supposed to hit the ground and be struck by the boot at the same time.

A dropped goal attempt should always be encouraged, for two reasons:

(i) if you get the ball between the uprights, it's worth three points.

(ii) if you don't, it's worth a few minutes' rest.

66

7. The place

On this occasion the ball is stationary, resting upon the ground after the kicker has spent ages digging up the grass with his heel to tee-up the ball.

Everyone likes to watch the expert place-kicker – everyone except the head groundsman.

8. The hack

Mostly used by people who have turned to rugby after playing soccer. With this type of kick, the ball is booted in the direction that the kicker is facing, no matter which way he's playing.

This kick is, of course, frowned upon by the pundits, but it can be a very effective weapon to have in your kicking armoury.

Some accomplished users of this kick can, with a thunderous hack, wind their opposite number from fifteen yards.

Rugby Terms Explained

As in every sport, correct terminology is important if you, the rugby duffer, wish to bluff your way conversationally through the after-match club bar appraisal of the game.

1. Scrummage

An organized group of forwards from both sides with heads down getting together to talk about the inadequacies of their backs.

2. Ruck

The term used to describe a punch-up when the ball is on the ground.

3. Maul

Same as a ruck punch-up, but the ball is not on the ground.

4. Foul play

The incident seen only by the referee when he feels it's about time he blew up for something.

5. The line-out

A touch-line confrontation in which the referee likes to ensure at least a yard between the sides before they start punching each other.

6. Lying-on

A term used to describe the action of a player who has about fifteen players on top of him and the ball underneath.

8. Advantage

What occurs when a player in your side has a blackmail hold over the ref.

7. Tackle

What happens when a player without the ball can't get out of the way of a player with the ball.

72

9. Mark

A bruised, dented area of flesh or bone received while trying to catch a high ball.

10. Conversion

A kick aimed at increasing a very lucky four points into an undeserved six.

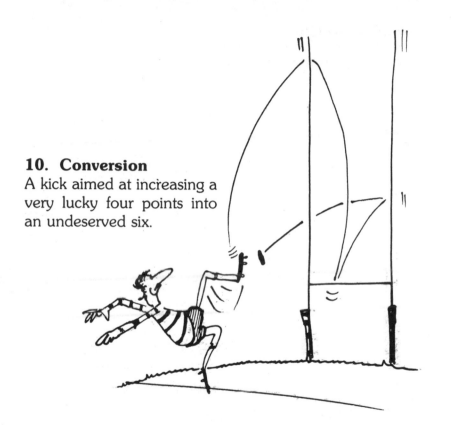

11. In goal

The area between the goal line and the dead-ball line where the grass is always greenest.

73

13. Binding
Stuff used to hold ears on.

14. Peeling-off
Cabaret at club stag party.

12. Drop-out
Description of a typical ex-university third XV centre.

15. Ball-carrier
Chap in crowd who sneaks off with the ball after it has been kicked into touch.

Understanding the commentator

One of the great delights about watching rugby is the tremendous pleasure we fans get from being rude to the players as they do their best out on the field of play.

Shouting at your star outside half 'Yer playin' like a geriatric three-legged fairy' is great sport and part of the real joy of rugby; but have you ever stopped to spare a thought for that band of un-sung heroes who can't hurl snide abuse at our sweaty friends? Yes, the radio and TV commentators. They have feelings like us too, you know, though they have to be much more subtle than us ordinary fans.

But they do it just the same.

As a poor innocent duffer, new to the game, you probably don't realize that the commentators speak in coded clichés. We experienced fans have known for years what they mean. For instance . . .

'They play a very committed type of rugby'
They're the dirtiest bunch of thugs I've ever seen.

'His interpretation of the new laws was interesting'
I didn't have a clue what the ref was supposed to be doing.

'They try to keep the ball tight up front'
The backs are rubbish.

'They play open, running rugby'
They're scared stiff of being tackled with the ball.

'His contribution often goes unnoticed'
The ref should have sent him off in the first half.

'His tactical kicking often keeps him out of trouble'
He can't pass.

'He plays with great tactical awareness'
He's managed to avoid tackling anyone all afternoon.

'That's only the second time I've seen that type of tackle'
The first was during an SAS raid.

'He's a very underrated player'
... according to his mother.

'He's a great motivator'
He's the big mouth of the team.

'He models his game on his hero'
Attila the Hun.

'They are unable to field a full-strength team today'
Half the pack are still drunk from last night.

'Off the field he's very sociable'
Last night he was as sociable as a newt.

'He's playing out of position this week'
He's rubbish and they're giving him one last chance.

'He's playing with a new confidence in his own ability'
He's realized his deputy is rubbish too.

'He seems to have made the position his own'
His father's just been elected chairman of the Selection Committee.

79

'His pace is deceiving'
I didn't know he was that slow.

'He had a season out of the game'
It would have been two seasons but he had full remission.

'He thinks about the game'
He's the slowest back they've got.

'He almost got an international cap'
... but the selection committee wouldn't accept his bribe.